E-Mail

Davinder Singh Minhas

RISING SUN

RISING SUN
an imprint of
New Dawn Press

NEW DAWN PRESS GROUP
New Dawn Press, Inc., 244 South Randall Rd # 90, Elgin, IL 60123
e-mail: sales@newdawnpress.com
New Dawn Press, 2 Tintern Close, Slough, Berkshire, SL1-2TB, UK
e-mail: ndpuk@newdawnpress.com
           sterlingdis@yahoo.co.uk

New Dawn Press (An Imprint of Sterling Publishers (P) Ltd.)

A-59, Okhla Industrial Area, Phase-II, New Delhi-110020
e-mail: sterlingpublishers@touchtelindia.net
           Ghai@nde.vsnl.net.in

Printed at Sterling Publishers Pvt. Ltd., New Delhi

Contents

Contents

1. Introduction

E-mail is the short form of **e**lectronic **m**ail. It is a transmission of messages and file via communications network, such as a local area network or the Internet, usually between computers. Today, e-mail enables administrators, teachers and students to communicate with millions of Internet users all over the world. It has become the fastest and cheapest way to exchange text and messages.

People have been using various means to communicate with each other for thousands of years.

Fire was used as a means of communication in many parts of the world. In 1588, a chain of bonfires was used to send warning signals from one end of the country to the other. In India, kings and emperors stationed relay horses to send messages from one part to another.

Pigeons have been used to send letters and messages from time immemorial.

In AD 1, the first postal service was started by China, Persia and the Roman Empire. Messages were written on scrolls and carried on horse-backs, or by ships. In such cases, messages would take weeks to arrive because of the long distances. Later, armed mail coaches were used. The mail started to be sent by train in the 19th century, making the postal service much cheaper to use. The first air mail service began in 1918, between Washington DC, and New York. Letters and packages could be sent across the two cities in just two days.

In 1837, messages could be sent over long distances very quickly by the invention of telegraph. A telegraph message could travel between the continents in a few minutes.

Ray Tomlinson developed the first email application for the ARPANET in 1971, consisting of a program called SNDMSG for sending mail, and a program called READMAIL for reading mail. In the 1980s messages were exchanged between computers in offices and universities that had been linked together. By 1990, e-mail had gone worldwide and had evolved as the most efficient means of communication.

The number of e-mail users and e-mail messages has grown phenomenally during the past few years, as indicated by this graph.

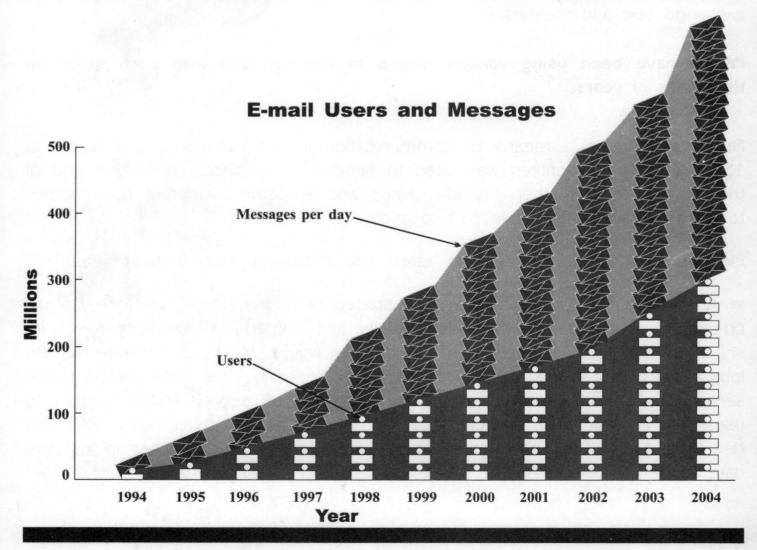

Now, let us take an example to compare the process of sending a message via the **Internet** or by **sending a letter by post**.

E-mail

Just type the address, compose your message and press the **Send** button.

Sending a Letter by Ordinary Post

First get a headed notepaper, find an envelope, go to the Post Office to buy the stamps, get a printout of the letter if it is typed, put it in an envelope and go to the postbox to drop the letter.

Simple mail could take a day, or two days, (or three or...) for the post to arrive, whereas the e-mail could be delivered in a matter of seconds, or a few minutes.

Some Advantages of E-mail

1.   E-mail is extremely fast. One can receive a message in a matter of seconds after it has been sent, irrespective of the geographic location of the sender and the recipient. You cannot find a better medium than the e-mail.

2.   When you send an e-mail message, the person you send it to does not have to be on the computer at that time to receive it. Mail can be collected whenever the person chooses to log on to his computer network or mail server.

3. You can send a message to a group of people at a low cost, quickly and easily as you can send to one person.

4. You can send documents, graphics, sound files, or any file as an attachment along with your e-mail.

5. There is no charge for sending and receiving e-mail, the only charge you need to pay is to your Service Provider. There is no extra payment even if a long message is sent or the message has to travel to the remotest corner of the world.

E-mail Programs

An e-mail program is used to create, send, receive, forward, store, print, and delete messages. When you receive an e-mail message, your Internet Service Provider's software places the message in your personal **mailbox.** Your mailbox is a storage location usually residing on the computer that connects you to the Internet, such as the server operated by your ISP. A server that contains user's mailboxes and associated e-mail messages is called a **Mail Server.**

The two of the most popular e-mail programs are **Outlook Express** and **Hotmail**.

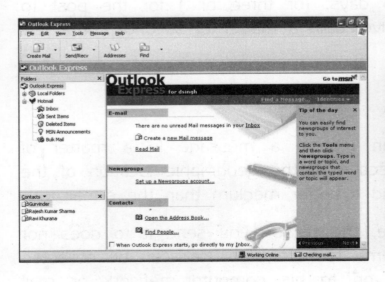

How E-mail Travels

The computers have to be linked together so that the e-mail message can travel.

1. An e-mail message is typed by the sender on his computer.

2. The message has an address, so that it can be sent directly to the right address.

3. The message is sent to a server which is connected to the Internet.

Server

4. The e-mail is then sent to a router by the server. The router sends the message to another router. Routers are connected to each other by telephone lines and cables.

5. The message is sent from one router to another until it reaches at the correct one.

6. The e-mail is finally passed by the router to the server. When the recipient's computer is connected to the server, the message can be displayed.

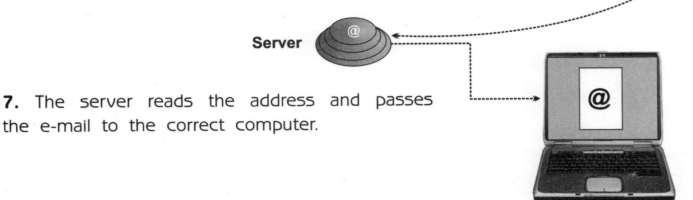

Server

7. The server reads the address and passes the e-mail to the correct computer.

Sometimes routers are too busy, or not working. In such cases, the e-mail messages are sent via other working routers.

How Computers Exchange Information

You need to have a set of rules like **protocol**, which determines how the information is to be sent. Internet Protocol (IP) is the most important protocol used on the Net. It specifies that the information sent between computers, servers and routers must be broken down into 'packets' of data.

What are Packets?

Packets are the small chunks which are broken by the Net while sending the e-mail message from one computer to another. Each packet contains the address of the destination computer. The messages are put back together to form the e-mail message, when this message reaches the designated computer.

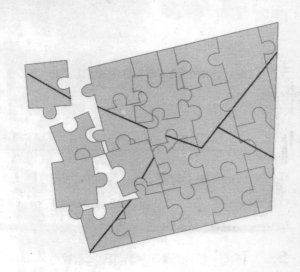

2. Features of E-mail

E-mail Address

If you have an e-mail address, you can send e-mail messages anywhere around the world. All e-mail users have their own, unique e-mail address. The messages are sent to the right computer because of the uniqueness of the address.

Parts of E-mail Address

An **e-mail address** is a combination of a user name and a domain name that identifies the user so he or she can receive messages. Your **user name** is a unique combination of characters that identifies you, and it must differ from other user names located on the same mail server. **Domain name** is the location of the person's account on the Internet.

An e-mail address consists of two parts (User name or Domain name) separated by the @ symbol. @ means at.

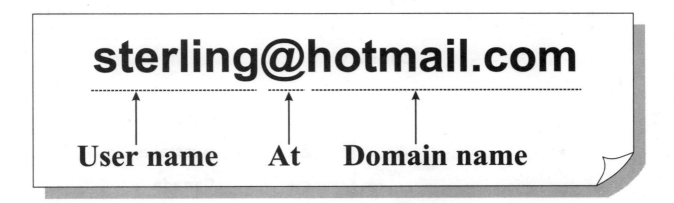

An e-mail address cannot use commas, spaces or brackets. Instead, hyphens and underscores can be used.

Domain Name

The **domain name** is separated into two parts by the period (.), and it is the location of the person's account on the Internet.

Types of Domain Name

The last few characters in an e-mail address shows the kind of organization the domain belongs to. These characters also shows the name of the country a person belongs to.

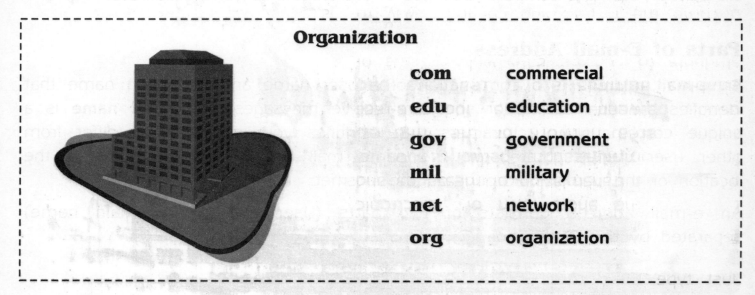

Organization

com	**commercial**
edu	**education**
gov	**government**
mil	**military**
net	**network**
org	**organization**

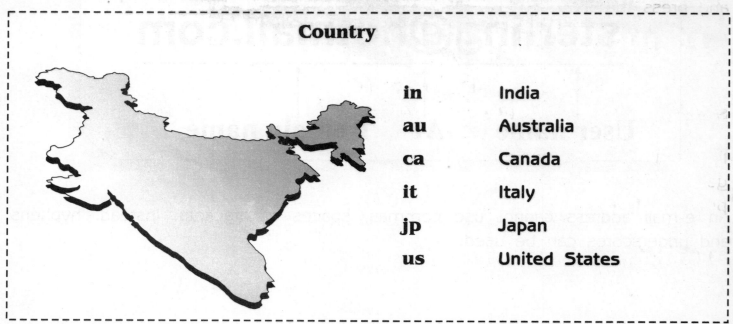

Country

in	**India**
au	**Australia**
ca	**Canada**
it	**Italy**
jp	**Japan**
us	**United States**

Selecting an E-mail Address

While creating an e-mail account the server will let you choose a user name. Your user name should be separate and has to be the name that hasn't already been chosen by anyone else. So, it is recommended that you use a combination of letters and numbers.

For example, a user name Rahul Bajaj, whose server has a domain name of hotmail.com, might select r_bajaj as his user name. If hotmail.com already has r_bajaj *(for Rajiv Bajaj)*, Rahul would have to select a different user name, such as rahulbajaj or rahul_bajaj. Many users select a combination of their first and last names so that others can remember it easily.

Finding an E-mail Address

The e-mail addresses of friends or colleagues can be found with the help of Web sites. Although there is no central listing of e-mail addresses but there are many places on the Web that help you in searching for e-mail addresses. Some of the Web sites are:

people.yahoo.com

www.bigfoot.com

INTERESTING E-MAIL ADDRESSES

Amitabh Bachchan - abachan@hotmail.com

Salman Khan - salman_khan_@hotmail.com

Bill Gates - billg@microsoft.com

Sunny Deol - sunny_9876@hotmail.com

Feedback on Zee TV - response@zeenetwork.com

E-mail Features

When you are writing an e-mail message, you have to deal with several parts of message, like **To:**, **Cc:**, **Bcc:** and **Subject**.

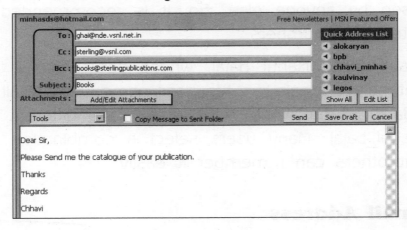

To:

Address of the person to whom you are sending the message.

Cc:

Cc stands for **carbon copy**. The field in an e-mail header that names additional recipients for the message.

Bcc:

Bcc stands for **blind carbon copy**. The field in an e-mail header that names additional recipients for the message. It is similar to carbon copy (Cc:), but the names do not appear in the recipient's message. Not all e-mail systems support Bcc:, in which case the 'hidden' names will appear.

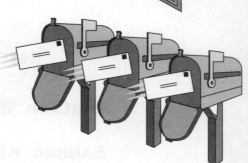

Subject:

With the help of subject, recipients can identify the contents of the message.

Books

The Button Bar

The button bar basically contains shortcuts to certain menu functions.

New Message

Pressing this button allows you to write a new e-mail to someone by invoking the e-mail authoring program.

Reply

This button will allow you to send a reply to someone who sent you an e-mail.

Reply to All

Sometimes you will receive an email of which you are not the only recipient. Pressing this button allows you to reply to all of the email addresses from that e-mail.

Forward

This button will help you to send forward a message, which you have received, to someone else.

Send and Receive

Pressing this button will serve two functions. It will query your mail server and receive any new e-mail that might be waiting for you, and it will send any pending messages, that you have authored, to your e-mail server.

Delete

This button allows you to delete the selected message.

Print

Some times you might want to keep a copy of the message with you. In such case this button (print) allows you to take a printout if the system is connected to the printer.

3. Sending or Receiving E-mail

Receiving an E-mail Message

Your e-mail messages can be received any time whether your computer is turned on or not. If your computer is not on at the time of receiving mail, your Internet Service Provider will store the messages in the mailbox for you. Whenever you turn on your computer, you will get your message from the mailbox.

Whenever you check your new message, you would not be checking the message from your computer, but from the mailbox of the service provider's computer, through your computer. That is why you can check your mail from anywhere, whether from your computer at home or from the computer of your friend at some other part of the country. This also allows you to check your messages while traveling.

Check Your Message Regularly

You should check your messages regularly, if possible, and delete the unnecessary ones because if your mailbox gets too full, some of your messages may be deleted by your service provider or there is a possibility of getting new messages very late.

Sending an E-mail Message

To make a reply to a mail that you receive or for exchanging ideas, you can send an e-mail message.

Composing an E-mail Message

There are some common e-mail terms that you will use while composing the message.

You can use your keyboard to type in a message in the message box window. Click on the message box area with the mouse. A flashing insertion point will appear which indicates where any character you type will appear.

If you make any mistake while typing a character, you can delete or remove the character by pressing the **Delete** key or **Backspace** key.

You can also edit your text by adding or deleting the character. It is done by moving the flashing insertion point (cursor) at any place on the message. The insertion point can be moved with the help of the arrow keys.

Formatting Text

You can change the style and size of the text in most of the e-mail programs.

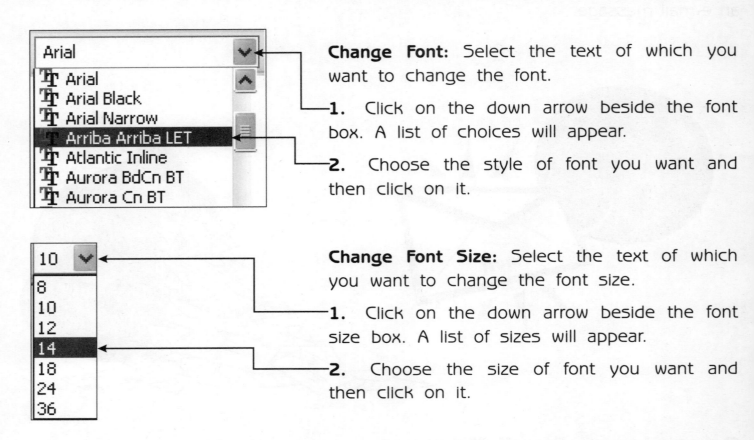

Change Font: Select the text of which you want to change the font.

1. Click on the down arrow beside the font box. A list of choices will appear.

2. Choose the style of font you want and then click on it.

Change Font Size: Select the text of which you want to change the font size.

1. Click on the down arrow beside the font size box. A list of sizes will appear.

2. Choose the size of font you want and then click on it.

You should compose your e-mail message when you are not connected to the Internet or in offline position. After composing your messages, you can connect to the Internet and send the messages all at once. This can save your money since you do not have to pay for the time you spend composing messages.

Smileys

Also called an **emoticon**, it is an expression of emotion typed into a message using standard keyboard characters. These characters look like human faces when you turn them sideways. For example, a **:-)** emoticon indicates that the message is meant as a joke and should not be taken seriously.

Abbreviation

Abbreviations are commonly used as a shorthand in e-mails. It is used to save time while typing.

Shouting

To use ALL CAPITAL LETTERS in an e-mail is annoying and very hard to read. This is called shouting. A word can be more acceptably emphasized by placing it between *asterisks* or _underscores_. E-mail messages should always use upper and lower case letters.

Bounced Message

Bounced message is a message informing the user that an e-mail could not be delivered to its intended recipients. The failure may be due to an incorrectly typed e-mail address or a network problem.

Signature

Signature is a pre-written text file appended to the end of an e-mail message that is used as a closing or an end to the message. It typically contains the sender's name and address, but may contain any kind of text that is repetitively sent.

Address Book

In the e-mail program, the Address Book is a utility that enables users to store and retrieve e-mail address and other contact information. It saves you from having to type the same address over and over again.

Attachment

A file (or group of files) that is included (or 'attached') with an e-mail message is called an 'Attachment'. You can attach files through almost any popular e-mail program, such as Eudora or Outlook Express. Usually, this is accomplished by simply clicking on the 'attach file' button and then browsing through your computer system to find and select the desired file or image.

E-mail Virus

Virus is a potentially damaging computer program, which negatively affects or infects your computer without your knowledge and alter the working of the computer. Most viruses are harmless, but some can be destructive. The increased use of e-mail has accelerated the spread of computer viruses. With these technologies, computer users can easily share files and any related viruses along with it.

One of the most common way of virus entering your computer is through the attachment in an e-mail. Before you open or execute any e-mail attachment, you should ensure that the e-mail message is from a trusted source. A **trusted source** is a company or a person you believe will not send you a virus-infected file knowingly. You should immediately delete any e-mail received from an unknown source without opening or executing the attachment. Thus, you can protect your computer against virus if you follow the precautionary measures.

Virus Scanner

A virus scanner is an anti-virus program that you can use to check e-mail attachments for viruses. Virus scanner manufacturers regularly release updates that allow their programs to detect the latest known viruses. Always make sure your virus scanner is up-to-date.

4. Outlook Express

Outlook Express is an e-mail program which is developed by Microsoft. You can create, send, receive, forward, store, print and delete messages using an e-mail program.

Title Bar

It shows the name of the current folder.

Menu Bar

The **menu bar** is a special toolbar that displays the Outlook menu names. Each **menu** contains a list of commands which you can use to perform tasks.

Standard Buttons

A **toolbar** contains buttons, boxes and menus that allow you to perform tasks more quickly than using the menu bar and related menus.

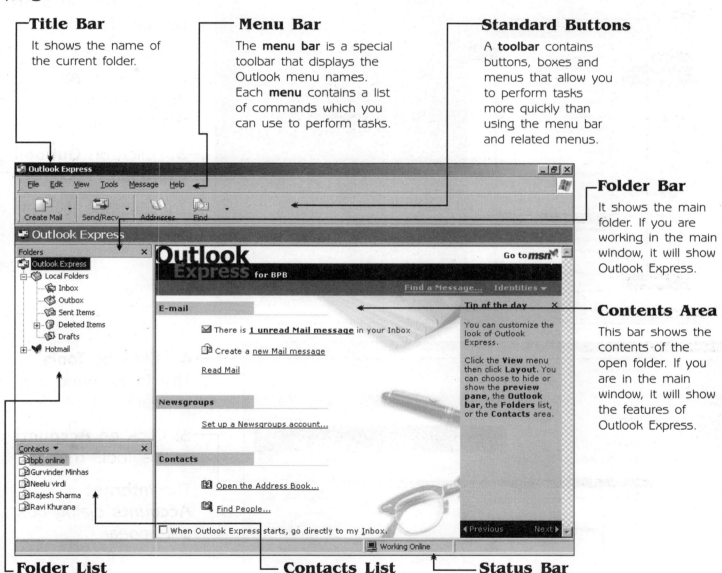

Folder Bar

It shows the main folder. If you are working in the main window, it will show Outlook Express.

Contents Area

This bar shows the contents of the open folder. If you are in the main window, it will show the features of Outlook Express.

Folder List

It shows the name of all the folders in which you can store e-mails. You can make or delete new folders according to your need. The main four folders are: Inbox, Outbox, Sent Items and Deleted Items.

Contacts List

This list shows the name of all the contacts which are saved in the Address Book.

Status Bar

Status bar is located at the bottom of Outlook Express window. This bar has information relating to the program being run.

Configuring E-mail Account with Outlook

You should have your mail account configured with Outlook so that you can check your mail and send replies. To configure your mail account perform the following steps:

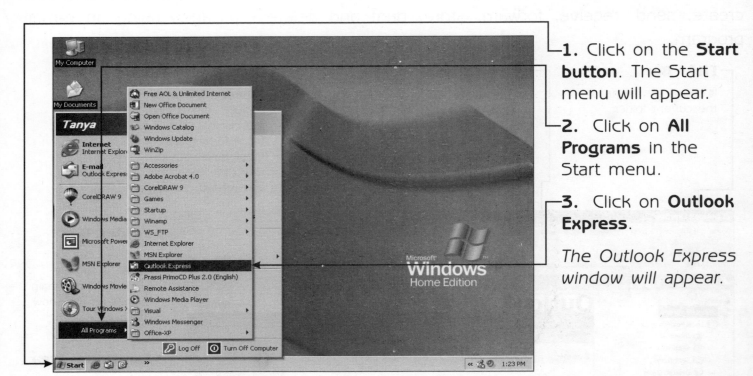

1. Click on the **Start button**. The Start menu will appear.

2. Click on **All Programs** in the Start menu.

3. Click on **Outlook Express**.

The Outlook Express window will appear.

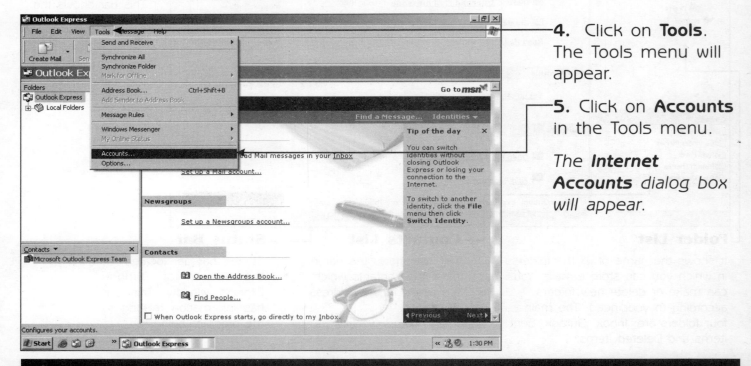

4. Click on **Tools**. The Tools menu will appear.

5. Click on **Accounts** in the Tools menu.

*The **Internet Accounts** dialog box will appear.*

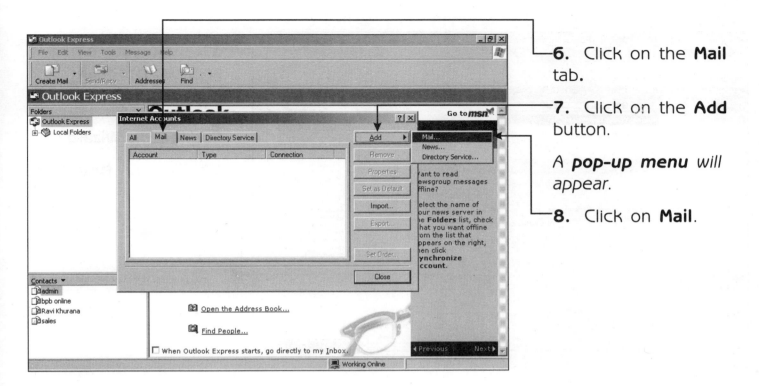

6. Click on the **Mail** tab.

7. Click on the **Add** button.

*A **pop-up menu** will appear.*

8. Click on **Mail**.

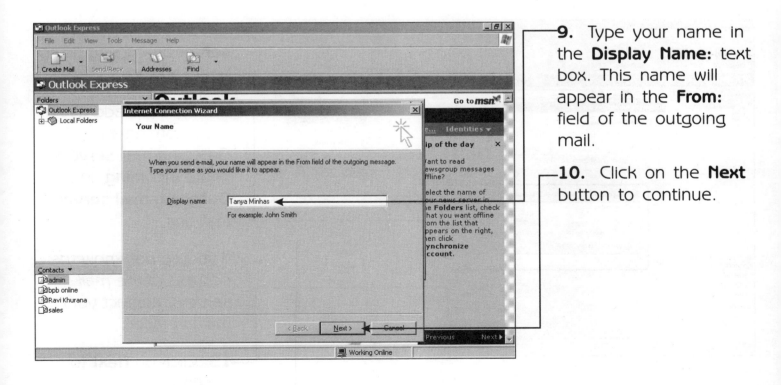

9. Type your name in the **Display Name:** text box. This name will appear in the **From:** field of the outgoing mail.

10. Click on the **Next** button to continue.

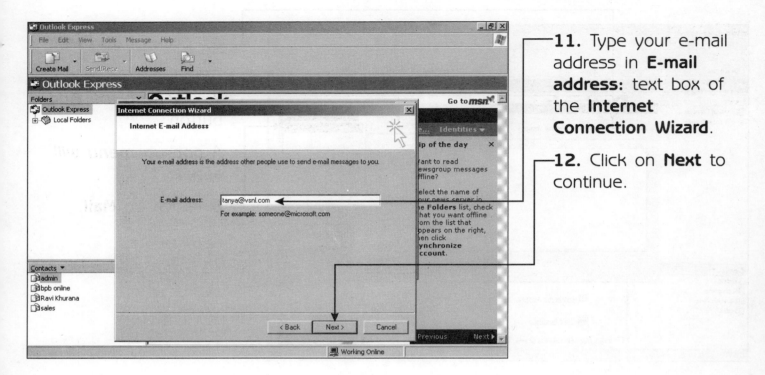

11. Type your e-mail address in **E-mail address:** text box of the **Internet Connection Wizard**.

12. Click on **Next** to continue.

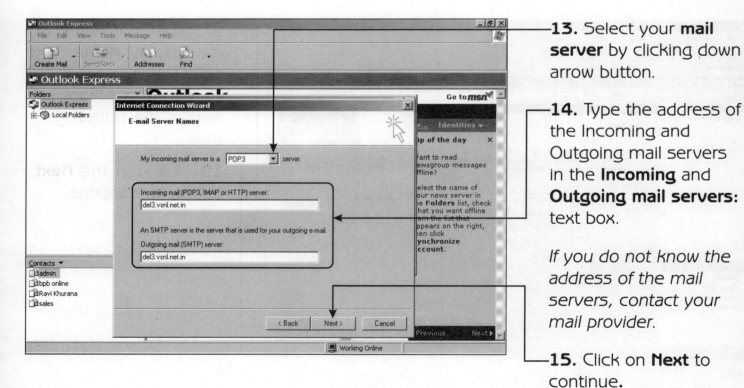

13. Select your **mail server** by clicking down arrow button.

14. Type the address of the Incoming and Outgoing mail servers in the **Incoming** and **Outgoing mail servers:** text box.

If you do not know the address of the mail servers, contact your mail provider.

15. Click on **Next** to continue.

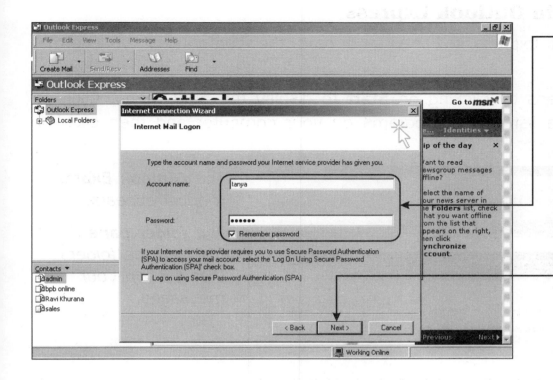

16. Type the account name and password, that your service provider has given you, in the **Account Name:** and **Password:** text box.

The password you type will appear in bullets (.)

17. Click on **Next** to continue.

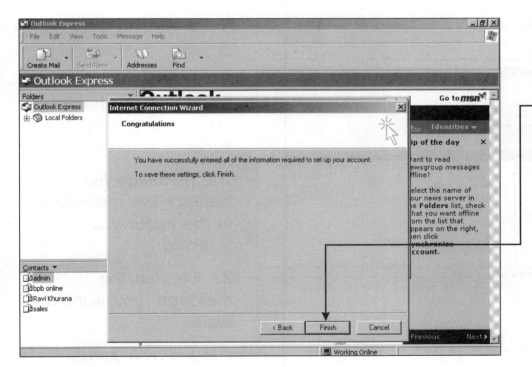

Your mail account in Outlook Express has been configured.

18. Click on **Finish**.

*The **Internet Accounts** dialog box will appear.*

19. Click on the **Close** button to close Internet Accounts dialog box.

Exchanging Mails in Outlook Express

You can start Outlook Express to open and read the contents of your e-mail messages.

1. Open Outlook Express by clicking on **Start** to display the Start menu. Click on **All Programs** to view a list of the programs on your computer and then click on **Outlook Express**.

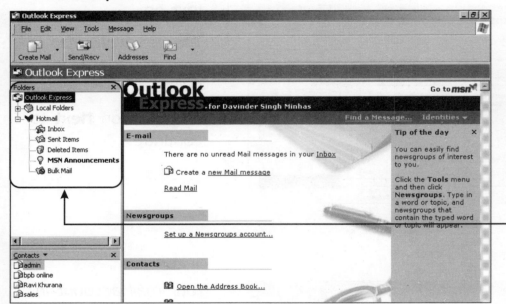

The **Outlook Express** window appears.

The **folder pane** displays the folders that contain your messages.

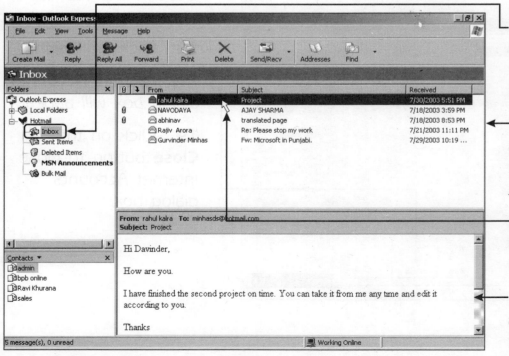

1. Click on the **folder** containing the messages you want to read. The folder is highlighted.

The **message list** displays the messages in the folder you selected.

2. Click on the **message** you want to read.

The **preview pane** displays the contents of the message.

Creating Messages

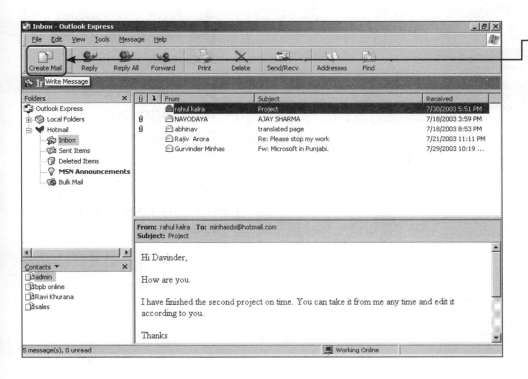

1. Click on **Create Mail** to write a new message.

*The **New Message** window appears.*

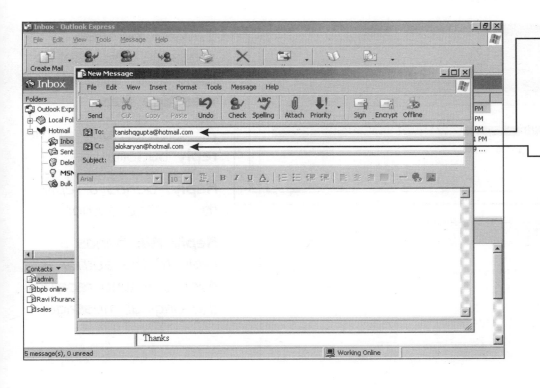

2. Type the e-mail address of the person you want to send the message to in **To:** box.

3. To send a copy of the message to a person who is not directly involved but would be interested in the message, type the person's e-mail address in the **Cc:** box.

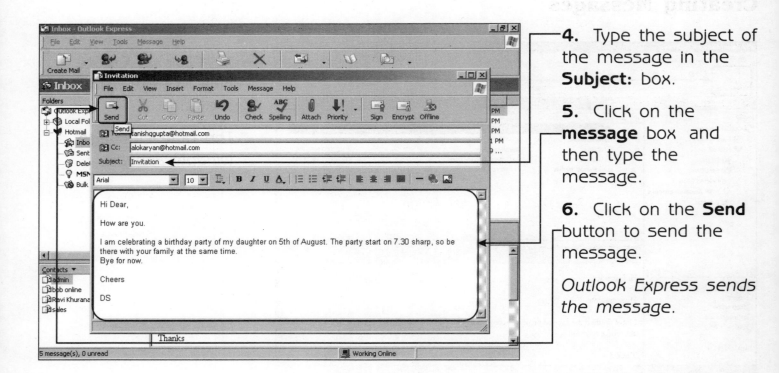

4. Type the subject of the message in the **Subject:** box.

5. Click on the **message** box and then type the message.

6. Click on the **Send** button to send the message.

Outlook Express sends the message.

Replying to the Messages

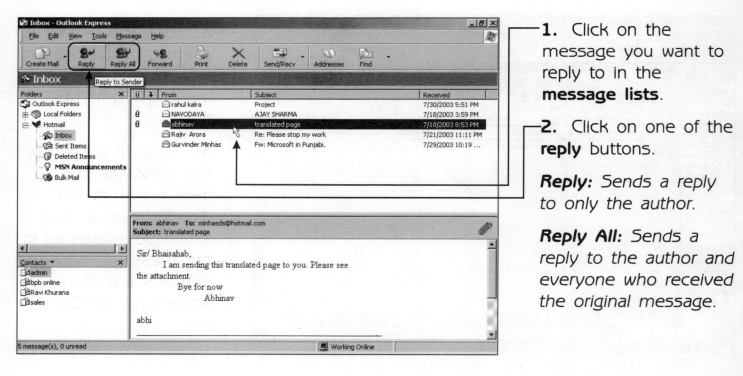

1. Click on the message you want to reply to in the **message lists**.

2. Click on one of the **reply** buttons.

Reply: *Sends a reply to only the author.*

Reply All: *Sends a reply to the author and everyone who received the original message.*

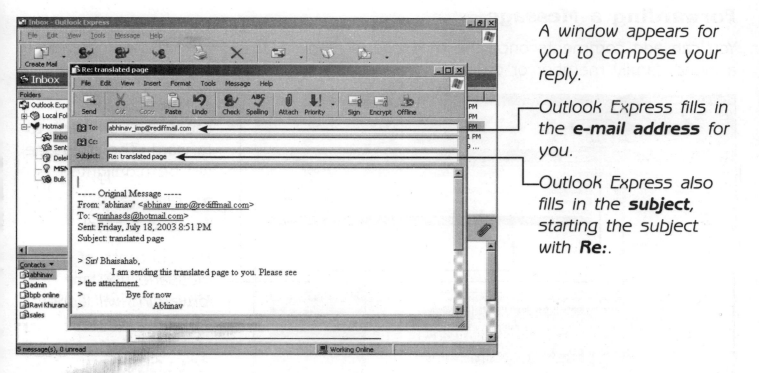

A *window appears for you to compose your reply.*

Outlook Express fills in the **e-mail address** for you.

Outlook Express also fills in the **subject**, starting the subject with **Re:**.

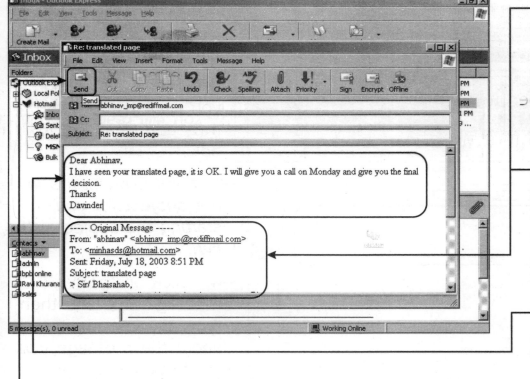

To help the reader identify which message you are replying to, Outlook Express includes a copy of the **original message**. This is called **quoting**.

3. By deleting the parts of the **original message** that do not directly relate to your reply, you can save the readers time.

4. Click on the message area and then type your reply.

5. Click on **Send** to send the reply.

Forwarding a Message

You can add comments once the message is read and then forward the message to a friend, family member or colleague.

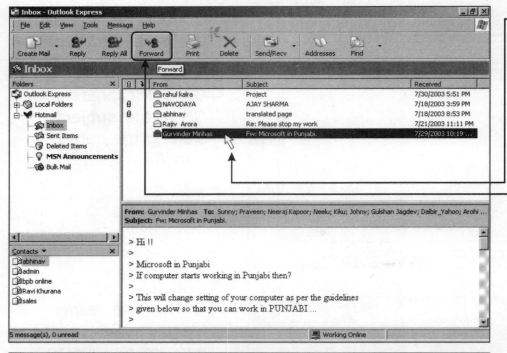

1. Click on the message you want to forward. The message will be highlighted

2. Click on the **Forward** button.

The contents of the message you are forwarding will appear in a new Window.

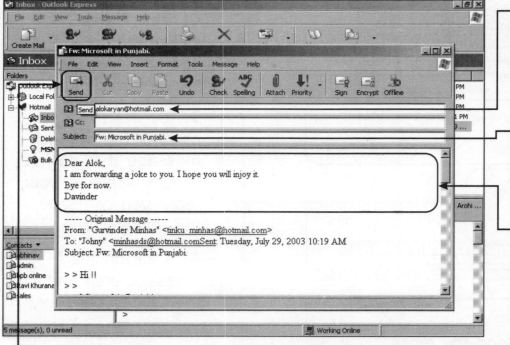

3. Type the e-mail address of the person you want to send the message to in the **To:** box.

*Outlook Express fills in the **subject** for you, starting the subject with **Fw:**.*

4. Click on the message area and then type any comments about the message you are forwarding.

5. Click on the **Send** button to forward the message.

Deleting a Message

You can delete message from your mail account which you no longer need.

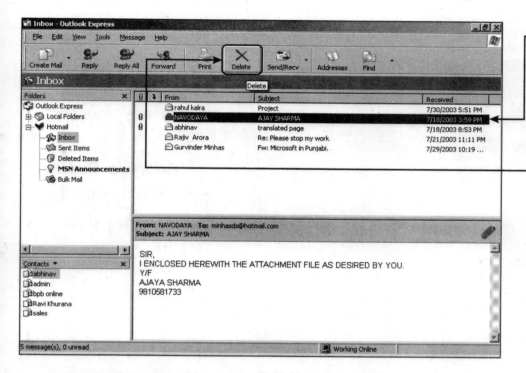

1. Click on the message you want to delete.

2. Click on the **Delete** button to delete the message.

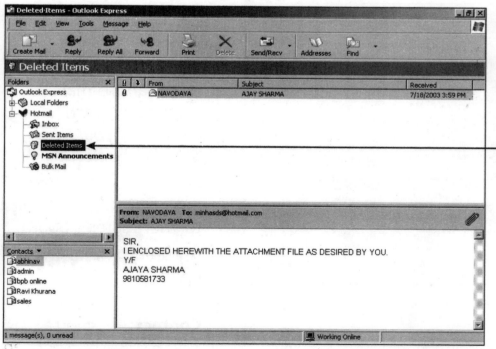

*Outlook Express removes the message from the current folder and places the message in the **Deleted Items** folder.*

Deleting a message from the Deleted Items folder will permanently remove the message from your computer.

The Address Book

You can use the Address Book to store e-mail addresses of people you frequently send messages to. By doing this, you can avoid typing mistakes when entering an e-mail address.

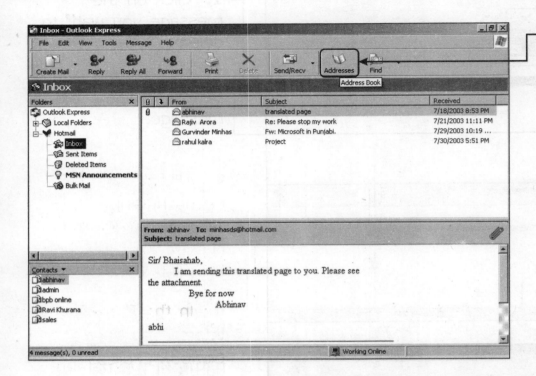

1. Click on the **Addresses** button to display the address book.

*The **Address Book** window will appear.*

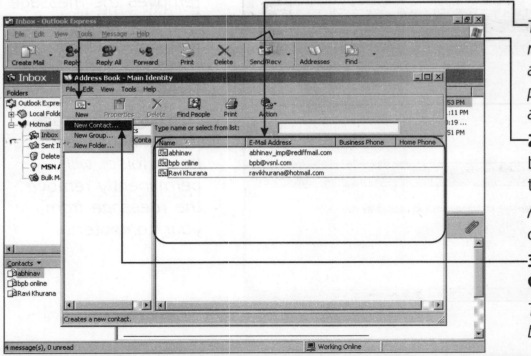

This area displays the name and e-mail address of each person in your address book.

2. Click on the **New** button to add a name to the address book.

A pop-up menu will open.

3. Click on **New Contact**.

*The **Properties** dialog box will appear.*

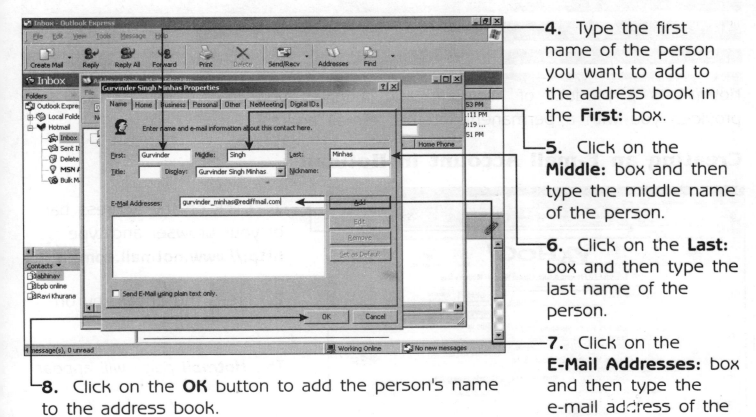

4. Type the first name of the person you want to add to the address book in the **First:** box.

5. Click on the **Middle:** box and then type the middle name of the person.

6. Click on the **Last:** box and then type the last name of the person.

7. Click on the **E-Mail Addresses:** box and then type the e-mail address of the person.

8. Click on the **OK** button to add the person's name to the address book.

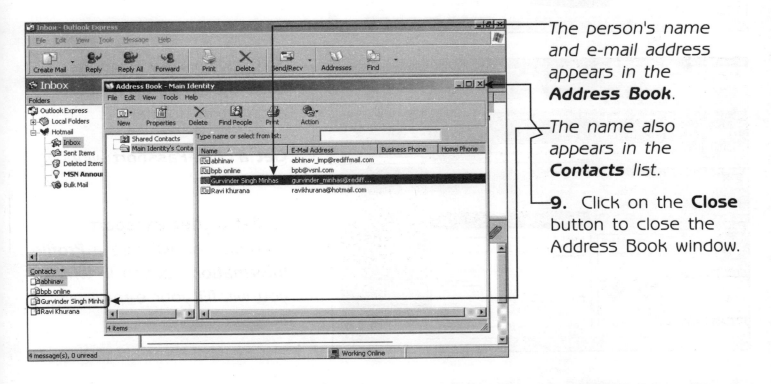

The person's name and e-mail address appears in the **Address Book**.

The name also appears in the **Contacts** *list.*

9. Click on the **Close** button to close the Address Book window.

5. Hotmail Account

Hotmail is a product of Microsoft and it gives you free e-mail service that provides you with a permanent Internet e-mail address.

Creating an E-mail Account in Hotmail

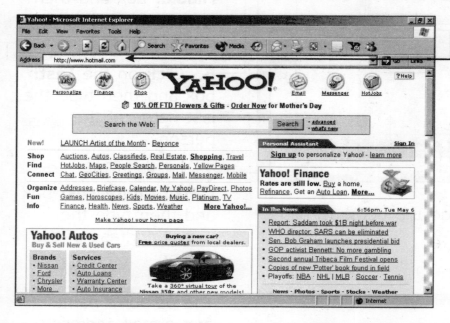

1. Click on the address bar of your browser and type **http://www.hotmail.com** in it.

2. Press the **Enter** key on the keyboard.

*The **Hotmail** page will appear.*

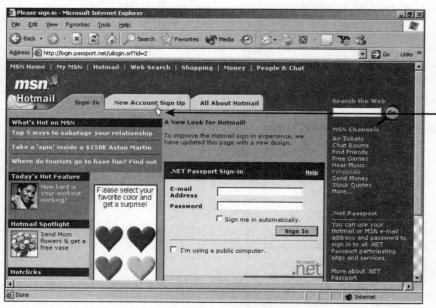

3. Click on **New Account Sign Up** to set up a new account in Hotmail.

***Get a .Net Passport** window will appear.*

*In **Get a .Net Passport** window, you will see a **Profile Information** section in which you will fill your e-mail account details.*

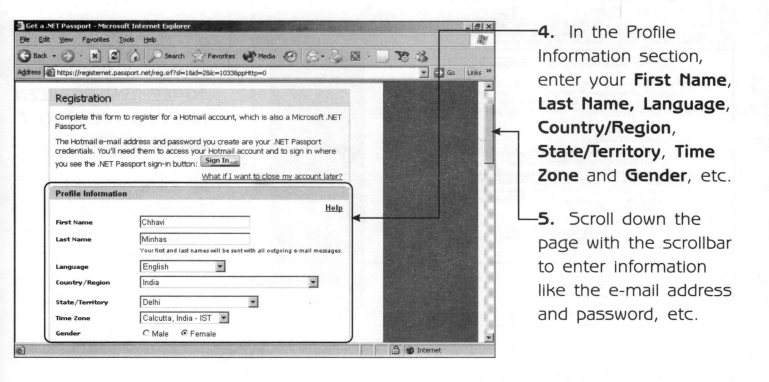

4. In the Profile Information section, enter your **First Name**, **Last Name, Language**, **Country/Region**, **State/Territory**, **Time Zone** and **Gender**, etc.

5. Scroll down the page with the scrollbar to enter information like the e-mail address and password, etc.

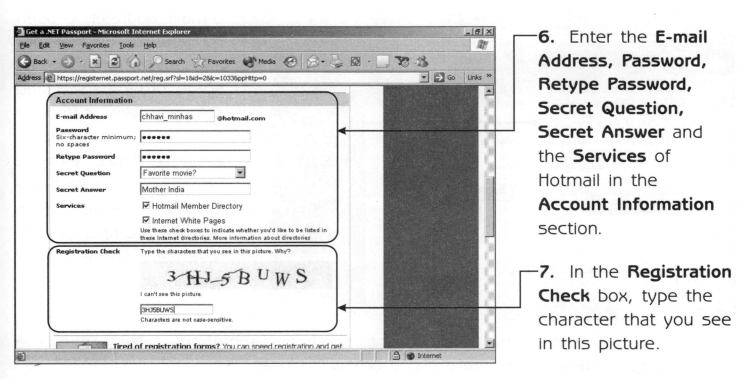

6. Enter the **E-mail Address, Password, Retype Password, Secret Question, Secret Answer** and the **Services** of Hotmail in the **Account Information** section.

7. In the **Registration Check** box, type the character that you see in this picture.

Scroll down with the scrollbar to reach the **Agreement** section.

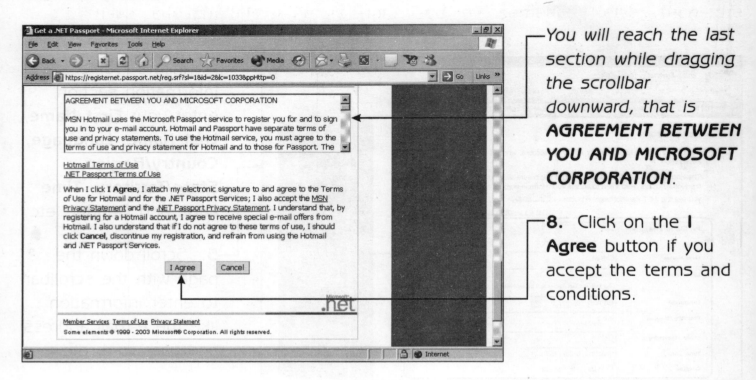

You will reach the last section while dragging the scrollbar downward, that is **AGREEMENT BETWEEN YOU AND MICROSOFT CORPORATION**.

8. Click on the **I Agree** button if you accept the terms and conditions.

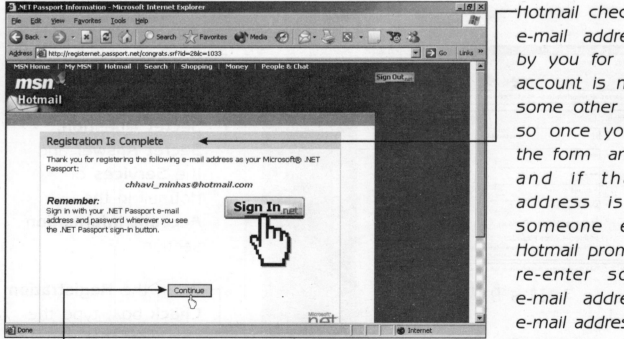

Hotmail checks that the e-mail address chosen by you for your e-mail account is not used by some other person and so once you complete the form and submit it and if that e-mail address is used by someone else, then Hotmail prompts you to re-enter some other e-mail address. If the e-mail address you

have chosen this time is not used by somebody else, then the **Registration Is Complete** dialog box will appear.

9. Click on **Continue** to proceed.

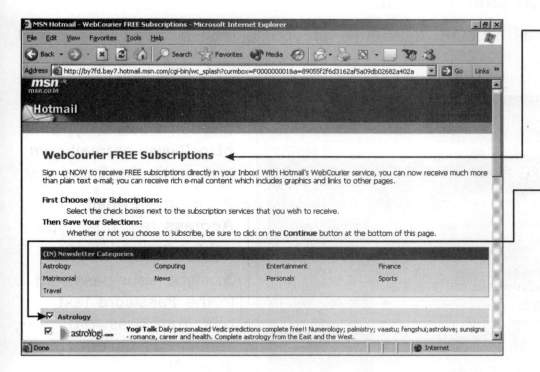

To subscribe for any of the interesting topics, **WebCourier Free Subscriptions** page will appear for you.

10. Click on the check box to select the topic of your interest.

Scroll down with **scroll bar** to see the rest of the page.

11. After selecting the checkbox of the topic, click on the **Continue** button.

Your account gets opened and gets displayed on the Hotmail page. This page is your mail page which will contain your e-mail address and the mails you receive on your account.

12. Click on **Inbox** to check the mails.

You will get a welcome mail from Hotmail.

Opening an E-mail Account in Hotmail

After creating your e-mail account, it is time for you to read or send your e-mail through Hotmail.

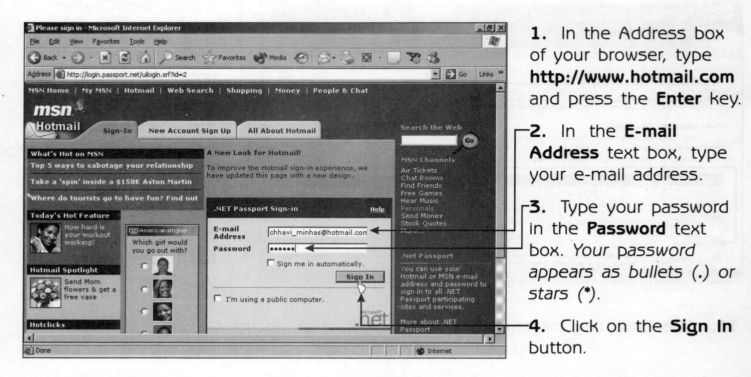

1. In the Address box of your browser, type **http://www.hotmail.com** and press the **Enter** key.

2. In the **E-mail Address** text box, type your e-mail address.

3. Type your password in the **Password** text box. *Your password appears as bullets (.) or stars (*).*

4. Click on the **Sign In** button.

The **Hotmail** *page gets displayed with your e-mail account.*

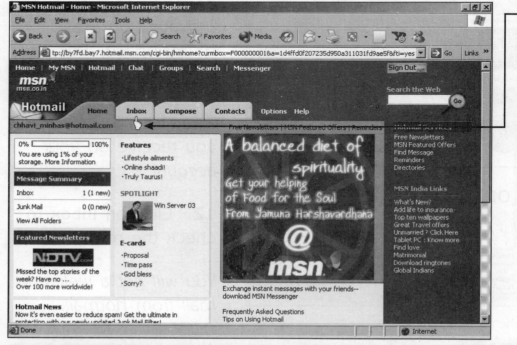

5. Click on the **Inbox** button in order to check your mails.

The **Inbox** *page will appear so that you can read your mails.*

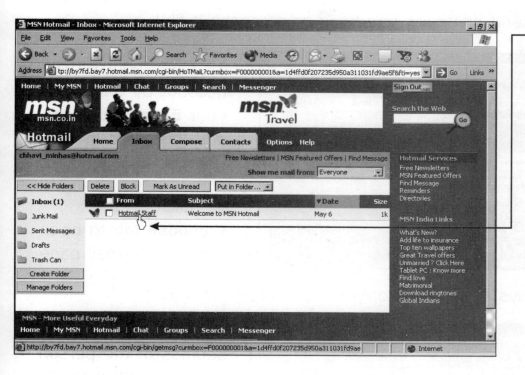

6. To read the mail, click on it with the mouse pointer.

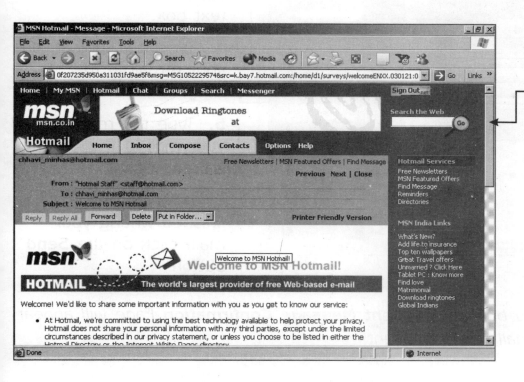

The e-mail you have selected will open.

To read the complete mail, just scroll down with the scroll bar.

Composing a New Mail

To send a mail to your friend or family, you have to compose it first.

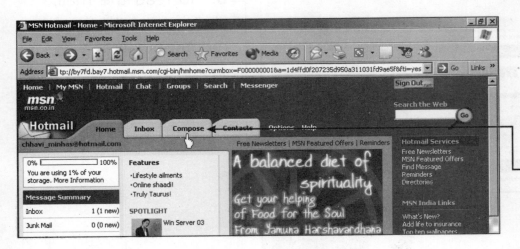

1. Open your e-mail account by entering your **E-mail Address** and **Password** in Hotmail.

2. Click on the **Compose** tab to open Compose e-mail page.

*The **Compose** page displays for you to compose or write your mail.*

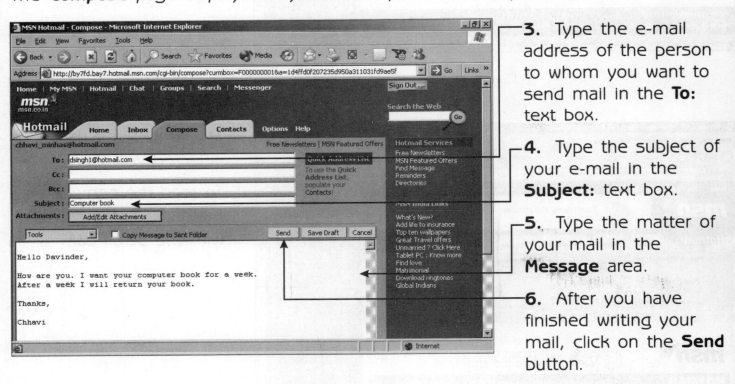

3. Type the e-mail address of the person to whom you want to send mail in the **To:** text box.

4. Type the subject of your e-mail in the **Subject:** text box.

5. Type the matter of your mail in the **Message** area.

6. After you have finished writing your mail, click on the **Send** button.

*After clicking on the Send button, the **Sent Message Confirmation** Page will appear to insure you that your mail has been sent.*